MW01622140

ELEPHANT SOUP?

By
Mary Ann
Castagnetta

Illustrations by
Mike Motz

Published by Elephant Soup, LLC., 2010
Printed in China

CPSIA Section 103(a) Compliant:
www.beaconstar.com/consumer
ID: K0116431
Tracking No.: K0312131-7025

Library of Congress Cataloging-in-Publication Data
ISBN-978-0-615-39269-1

Elephant Soup? - Author Mary Ann Castagnetta
Illustrator - Mike Motz

I dedicate this book to my beloved son, John,
who is always in my heart and on my mind,
My wonderful parents, Nella & Louie,
And my amazing husband, Eddie, always
loving, always supportive, always making me
laugh, my gratitude and love forever.

The day started out like any other day for John.
He jumped out of bed to get ready for school.

He had a hearty breakfast while his Mom and he talked and shared thoughts and ideas with each other, just as they did every day.

He went to school and always enjoyed seeing his friends in class.

At lunchtime he ate his sandwich, drank his milk and had some apple slices. His friend Tori was making such funny faces that he almost spit out some of his milk.

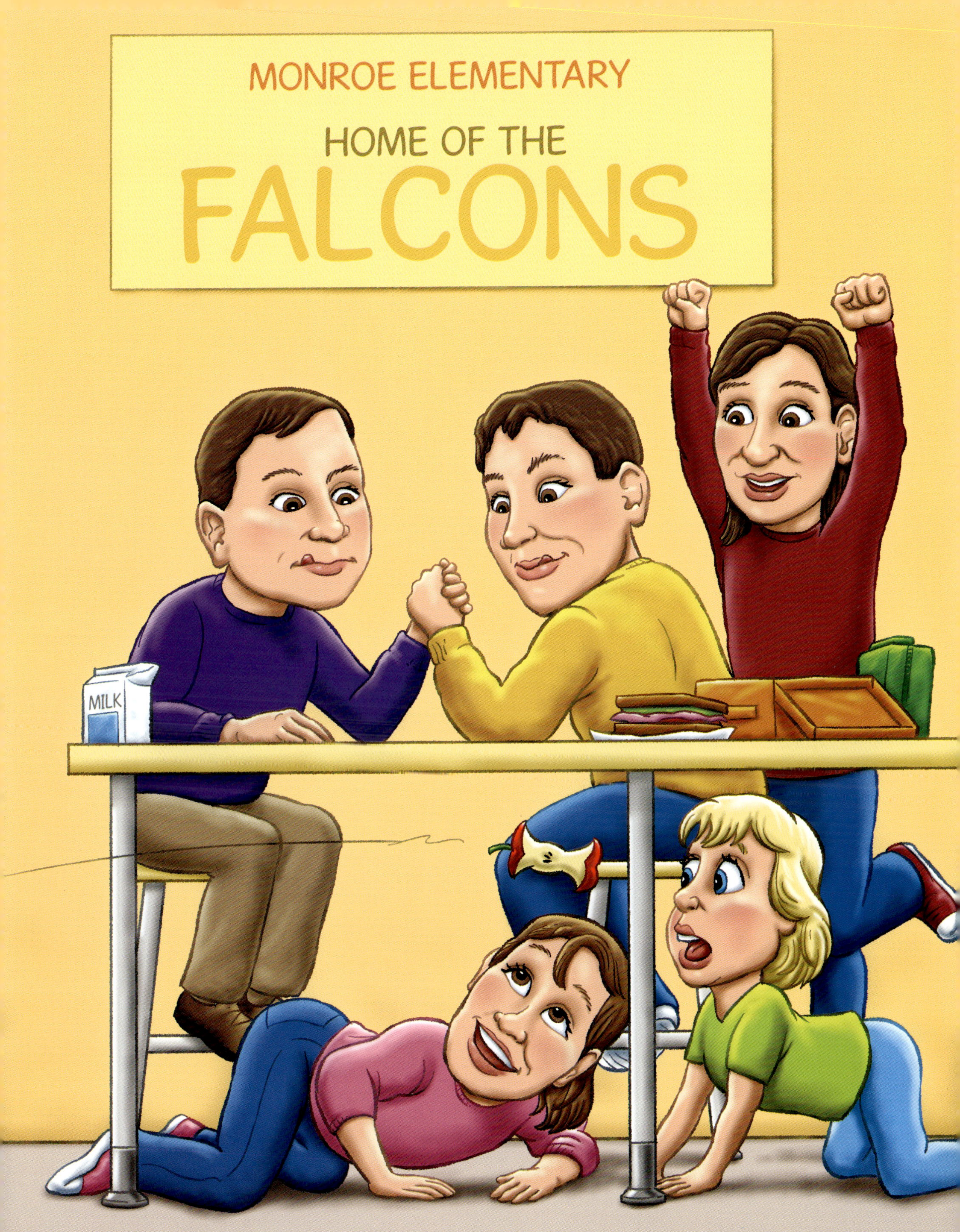

MONROE ELEMENTARY
HOME OF THE
FALCONS

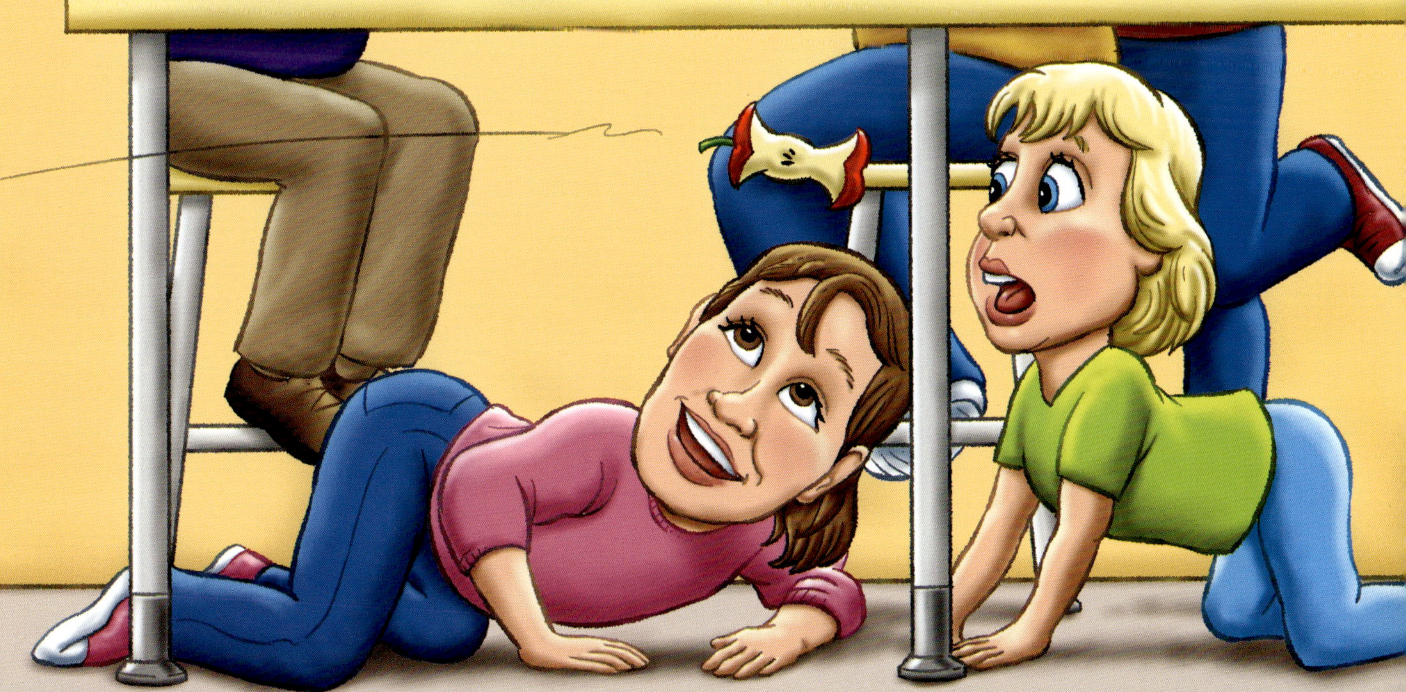
MILK

After school, as he was starting to walk home,
he started to feel very tired.
His throat was scratchy and his nose
was getting quite stuffy.

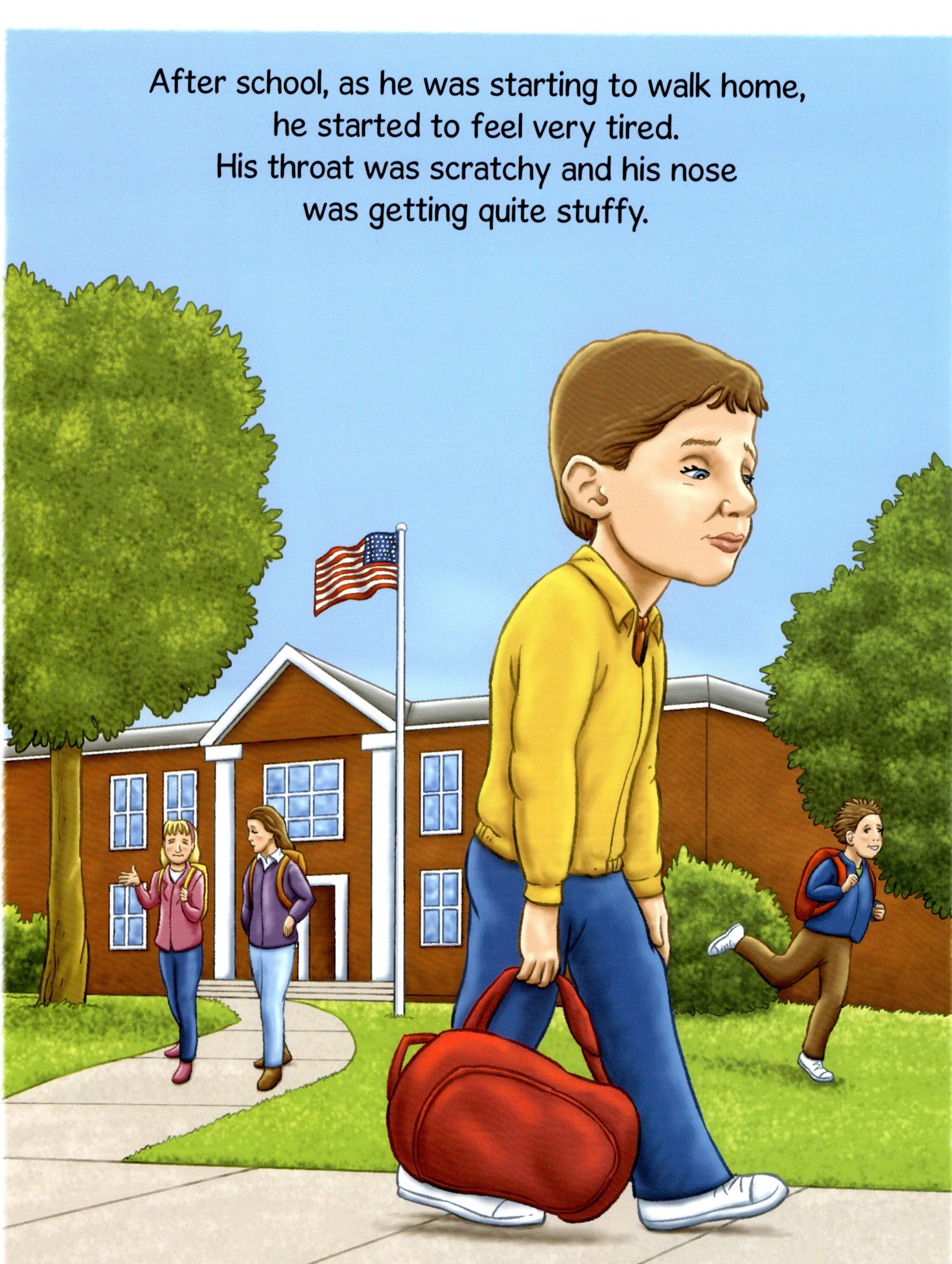

By the time John arrived home he knew he was sick! His Mom also knew the minute he walked through the door. "Oh my poor little boy", she said, "I think you need to get into your pajamas and get under the blankets. What do you think?" John was more than happy to do just that.

Once John was nice and cozy under the covers with his stuffed monkey, Chubbs, his Mom came in and said, "John, I just called Nana and told her you weren't feeling well. She is whipping up a batch of her wonderful Elephant Soup and will bring it over for you in a little while".

John sat straight up in bed. Did he hear correctly?
Elephant Soup?
How could that be? His Sweet Nana making Elephant Soup?
This must be a mistake! Surely Nana wouldn't hurt an Elephant!
And why would any one want to eat Elephant Soup? And WHERE would she even get an Elephant to make into soup?

Nana's SAFARIS

Did she go hunting for Elephants on a Safari? Did she capture one and tie it to the roof of her car and bring it home?

AISLE 5
ELEPHANTS
FRESH
LESS FILLING

Did she go to the Supermarket and find the aisle that sells Elephants and pick out the one she liked best?

Home
Sweet
Home
TOP STORIES

Did she order an Elephant from one of those shopping channels on television where they sell just about anything?

And just how big did the soup bowl have to be for an Elephant to fit in?

Oh no! This was too much for him to take!
He pulled the covers up to his nose
and held onto Chubbs hoping Nana had changed her mind.

John didn't want to hurt Nana's feelings, but there was
NO WAY WAS HE GOING
TO EAT ELEPHANT SOUP!
He didn't know what he should do, and then
THE DOORBELL RANG!!!!!

John’s Mom came into his room followed by Nana who was carrying a bowl of soup. “Hello my sweet John”, said Nana, “Here is some delicious soup I made just for you, with love”.

John had his eyes closed and was afraid to look, but he could smell the soup and boy did it smell delicious!!! Wait a minute!! John recognized that smell!! It smelled just like his Nana's Chicken Noodle Soup!!!

When he opened his eyes he saw Nana standing before him, holding a bowl that an Elephant could NEVER fit in. And when he looked into the bowl, he was so happy to see it was Nana's Chicken Noodle Soup!!
John looked at his Mom puzzled and said, "Mom, I thought you said Nana was making me Elephant Soup?"

"ELEPHANT SOUP"? John's Mom started laughing. "No Silly, I said she was making **L - F - N** soup. The **LFN** stands for **L**ove **F**rom **N**ana".

John and Nana and his Mom laughed and laughed over the mixup as John ate his...

Love From Nana Soup.

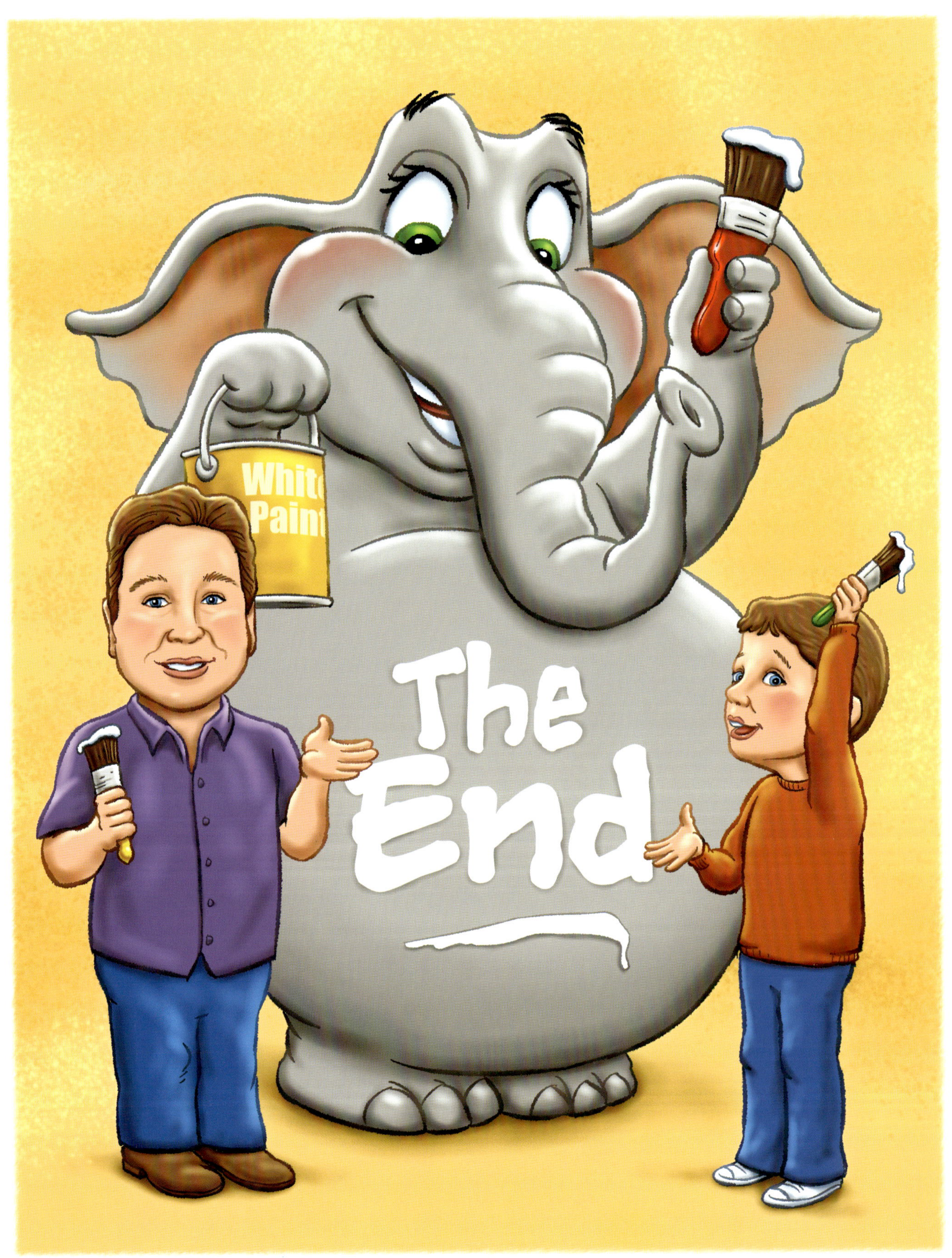
White
Paint
The End